STARS AR

LUCY DAWKINS

Published by Penteract Press, 2020
PenteractPress.com
PenteractPress@gmail.com
Twitter.com/PenteractPress

Edited and designed by Anthony Etherin

Typeset in Minion

Cover artwork: 'The Flammarion Engraving'
(artist unknown; from *L'atmosphère: météorologie populaire*
by Camille Flammarion, 1888)

Art opposite biography: 'Panorama'
by Lucy Dawkins, Anthony Etherin, and Clara Daneri

FIRST EDITION

ISBN 978-1-9998702-7-0

for Mom and Dad

Contents

TELESCOPE

The
poet,
like
a
telescope,
is
closest
to
distant
stars....

CORONAE

Go.
Far
at
sea,
no
rococo
coronae
star
a
fog.

FALLING STAR

A falling star is a raging, fatal assailant.

It is a flailing griffin,
tilting its nails.

Its snarl is lifting air.
Its tail is rattling rain.

A falling star is astral graffiti
in glaring satins.

Its altar is in transit.
I sit in its glinting flint.

When the Stars Are Falling

Sometimes, when the stars are falling,
one glides where a planet was. (I
oftentimes, when the stars are darling,
go melt in the dense dark, as the wax light
softens its shell.)
                           Free as a sea, night
comes with jewels, heaps a petal kiss
on the hiddenness. Red stars are starting
over in relentless arms. Agendas blink,
sometimes.
                    When the stars are falling,
others rise.
                    There's a star we ask things.

DIAMOND STAR

We
see
bare
stars:
fallen,
cracked
diamonds,
glowing
inside
space,
time
and
us.

STARDUST

Dust,
from
some
star
that
fell,
made
your
open
eyes.

WESTWARD

Westward
stars
weave
secrets,
traverse
deserted
stages;
affect
exaggerated
cascades....

DARK AFAR

Stars batch and mass.
Stars pack and stack.
Stars swarm, attach a clan, as sparks.

All stars pass.
Stars halt and crash.
Dark lava attacks and stars thrash back.

A vacant black afar hangs tall,
and arms and hands
catch stars that fall.

STARS ARE FALLING

Stars are falling.
A lag first learns
a stranger's flail.
Stars fill a range.

Far signals alter
a girl. Fears slant.
Real stars flag in
fair astral glens.

A large snarl fits
a fire's last gnarl.
All faster grains
flare. Stars align.

Fall and Rise

Star, yell a sad nil.

By name to me,
regal lips assert
star redness.

Tell arts, all afoot,
I too fall astral.

Let's send, err at stress,
a spillage remote;
many blind as alley rats....

Breathless

Stars:
crystalline
fragments,
transforming
astronomical
scarcity;
scarlet
hearts
thrashing
breathlessly...

Jewels

The
stars:
like
quiet
pixels,
calmly
delivering
blitzes
of
jewels.

Leap, Star!

Leap, star!

So my series is true,
I dip sky.

I skip!

I duet.

Rises rise,
my soar staple.

HOURGLASSES

Hourglasses
carefully
emptied
above
you...
I
see
stars
descend,
eternally
resplendent.

Satellites

Some satellites say
stars should stay stationary,
shelving spherical schemes,
suppressing stellar spiraling.

Some satellites suggest
solely satellites should swoop.

Seriously spiteful satellites say
stars shouldn't simmer,
shouldn't spark.

LOST ART

Lost
art,
here
bet
all...
Lo!
Star
there!
Be
tall!

SONATA

Tan
a
soon
near
star:
A
far
star,
neon
sonata.

Binoculars

Stainless binoculars
marshal distant stars.

Binoculars parse stadia,
establishing statuses,
understanding crystalline statues.

Starry nostalgia sustains ecstasy,
gestating fearsome tears.

Exact Stars

Giant stars shake sharp roars.

Small stars shape grave beams.

Dwarf stars blast weary space.

Frail stars again blaze flame.

Heavy stars smash space apart.

Stars Stumble

Stars (striking structures)
strangely stumble,
steeply stooping....

Strewn stars strain, strangled stiffly,
stimulating stellar storms.

Straggling stars stretch struggling stars;
strong stars strip stark stars....

Strict stars stabilize.

WISHES

Poets'
hearts
burn
with
sight...
　　Wish
　　upon
　　　the
　　brightest
　　　star!

BROKEN

A
star
explodes,
ejecting
quartz
flames
in
waves.
You're
heartbroken.

Ode

Time in it,
a star is spilt ink,
now angelic odes.

I rise, docile,
gnaw on knit lips.

Sir, at satin, I emit.

A Star Falls, Blissfully

Ancient
Stars
Tumble
And
Rupture.
Fiery
Arrows
Light
Loving
Skies.

Bright
Little
Islands
Slide,
Scarcely
Fathomed,
Under
Long,
Lofty
Yearning.

All the Time

Skies dip captive
                ice and fire,

dream the quilted
                air and orbs —

moons wax blankly
                now, but rise.

Stars are falling,
                all the time.

MADNESS

I
am
the
star
whose
fierce
madness
scorches
desperate
firmaments.

ASTRONOMER

Astronomer:
Celestial
observer,
radiant
galaxy,
naked
star,
mad
as
I.

Spheres

Suns supress
sleeplessness.

Spacious stars
stress superfluous spaces.

Stillness, stillness...

Strenuous strangeness
swallows spheres.

PULSAR

Rarer star,
appear far,
pour your simmer!

Rarer star,
unfamiliar pulsar,
flutter your shimmer!

Rarer star,
roar your nuclear thunder!
Utter your glimmer!

Last Star

That last star fell
down like dew's kiss.

That last star fell
down like some late,
lazy dusk that won't
quit your even tide.

That last star fell
down like dawn mist.

Notes on the Constraints

Each poem in this collection includes the word 'star' or its plural. Also:

Telescope is a 10-word poem

Coronae is a 10-word palindrome.

Falling Star is a lipogram, using only the letters in its title.

When the Stars Are Falling has lines that feature the same vowels, in the same order, while varying consonants (it is homovocalic).

Diamond Star has line letter counts 2-3-4-5-6-7-8-7-6-5-4-3-2.

Stardust is a 10-word poem using only 4-letter words (tetragrams).

Westward is a 10-word poem using only those letters on the left-hand (west) side of a qwerty keyboard (q to t, a to g, & z to v).

Dark Afar is a univocalic lipogram, avoiding the letters e, i, o, u & y.

Stars Are Falling has lines that are perfect anagrams of each other.

Fall and Rise is a palindrome.

Breathless is a 10-word poem using only words that contain the letters s, t, a, & r.

Jewels is a 10-word poem using every letter of the alphabet at least once (it is a pangram).

Leap, Star! is a palindrome by pairs of letters.

Hourglasses has line letter counts 11-9-7-5-3-1-3-5-7-9-11.

Satellites is a tautogram, using only words that begin with s.

Lost Art is a 10-word redivider, whose first 5 words are together spelled the same as the second 5.

Sonata is a 10-word palindrome by pairs of letters.

Binoculars uses only words containing either 'sta' consecutively or 'ars' consecutively. Of the words included, only 'stars' has both of these properties.

Exact Stars uses only 5-letter words whose central letter is a.

Stars Stumble is a double tautogram, whose words begin with 'st'.

Wishes is a 10-word poem whose first 5 words are a perfect anagram of its second five words.

Broken is a 10-word pangram, using every letter of the alphabet at least one time.

Ode is a palindrome.

A Star Falls, Blissfully is an acrostic whose title is spelled out by the first letter of each word.

All the Time is a 100-letter poem whose four 25-letter lines employ words with corresponding letter counts.

Madness is a 10-word poem whose lines have letter counts of 1-2-3-4-5-6-7-8-9-10

Astronomer is a 10-word poem whose lines have letter counts of 10-9-8-7-6-5-4-3-2-1.

Spheres is a two-sided tautogram, whose words both begin and end in s.

Pulsar is a reverse tautogram, using only words that end in r.

Last Star is composed of only 4-letter words (tetragrams).

ACKNOWLEDGEMENTS

Many thanks to my mentor Anthony Etherin for all the revisions and rewrites, corrections, advice and encouragement. (And thank you, Clara, for letting me take up so much of his time!!)

Thanks to Rob McLennan for publishing 'Falling Star' on the Dusie blog.

Thanks to Mandy, Kara, Jen and Jessica, for your support, even when you don't know why I do this!

Most of all, thanks to Mom and Dad, for teaching me to love words and stars....

L. x

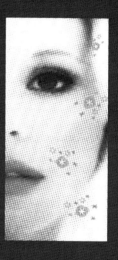

Lucy Dawkins is a model and experimental poetess. She tweets her poetry @lucykdawkins. She has had her poems published by Penteract Press and above/ground press. 'Stars Are Falling' is her first book.